Dear Reader,

I've read many fine books about me over the years. When I found this biography on a desk one night, I couldn't resist adding a few notes. (I never could hold back my opinions, to be honest!) I hope you find the extra details helpful in learning about me.

Your most humble servant,

N. Webster

Noah Webster's FIGHTING WORDS

Tracy Nelson Maurer

illustrated by
Mircea Catusanu

Edited by
Noah Webster, Esq.

M

MILLBROOK PRESS

MINNEAPOLIS

For Ann, who loves words too
–T.N.M.

To the most passionate reader I've known, my father
–M.C.

For America, as always —N.W.

ACKNOWLEDGMENTS
Special thanks to the Noah Webster House staff and the kind librarians at Amherst College, Minneapolis Public Library, New York Public Library, and Yale University. Thank you to the Society of Children's Book Writers and Illustrators for the research grant to visit those sites. Also, unabridged gratitude to Kendra Marcus, Carol Hinz and the Millbrook team, Ann Matzke, the Wordsmiths Writing Group, Candace Fleming, John Morse and Meghan Lunghi at Merriam-Webster, and my family for their countless words of encouragement.

Millbrook Press
A division of Lerner Publishing Group, Inc.
241 First Avenue North
Minneapolis, MN 55401 USA

For reading levels and more information,
look up this title at www.lernerbooks.com.

I pushed for America's first national copyright laws. Nice to see them still at work!

Main body text set in Breughel Com Roman 18/23. Typeface provided by Linotype AG.
The illustrations in this book were created using mixed media, including collage, digitally processed.
Additional images: *Engraving of Noah Webster* courtesy Wikimedia Commons, jacket flap; *Noah Webster*, 1823, by Samuel Finley Breese Morse provided by Mead Art Museum/Bridgeman Images, p. 37.

Library of Congress Cataloging-in-Publication Data

Names: Maurer, Tracy, 1965– author. | Catusanu, Mircea, illustrator.
Title: Noah Webster's fighting words / by Tracy Nelson Maurer ; illustrated by Mircea Catusanu.
Description: Minneapolis, MN : Millbrook Press, A division of Lerner Publishing Group, Inc., [2016] | Includes bibliographical references.
Identifiers: LCCN 2016019759 (print) | LCCN 2016033624 (ebook) | ISBN 9781467794107 (lb : alk. paper) | ISBN 9781512428391 (eb pdf)
Subjects: LCSH: Webster, Noah, 1758–1843—Juvenile literature. | Lexicographers—United States—Biography—Juvenile literature. | Educators—United States—Biography—Juvenile literature.
Classification: LCC PE64.W5 M28 2016 (print) | LCC PE64.W5 (ebook) | DDC 423.092 [B] —dc23

LC record available at https://lccn.loc.gov/2016019759

Manufactured in the United States of America
1-38476-20327-9/26/2016

Noah Webster was a proud American, even as a little boy.

"I began life . . . full of confidence in my own opinions," he once said.

< No one could argue with that.

Words! Numbers! They tickled young Noah. He learned to spell and count with his family at their home in West Hartford, Connecticut.

∧ My mother was my first teacher. I was lucky to have such a well-educated mother.

Noah

oh !

Noah read everything he could find.

In his opinion, his father's farm chores ~~could wait, especially if he had a new~~ ~~issue of the *Courant*.~~

REWRITE: He gladly helped with the farm chores even when he had a new issue of the **Courant**.

hmm...

The Connecticut Courant.

MONDAY, OCTOBER 29, 1764.   (Number 00.)

HARTFORD: Printed by THOMAS GREEN, at the Heart and Crown, near the North-Meeting-House.

School was a different story. Noah claimed that his old drafty schoolhouse had "no book for reading."

other

He also said that students spent most of
their time planning "roguish tricks."

At the age of fifteen, he convinced his parents to send him to Yale College.

There, he found countless books.

< And I tried to read them all!

He also found friends at Yale who would listen to his sharp opinions about King George's taxes . . .

. . . *Taxes on molasses!*

. . . *Taxes on sugar and paper!*

. . . *Taxes on paint, glass, and tea!*

But the American colonists had no say in the king's taxes.

Words flew, then bullets. The American Revolutionary War exploded in Massachusetts in 1775. Colonists fought to create an independent country, separate from Great Britain. Noah did not fire a single shot. Instead, he fought with his pen.

He wrote letters, speeches, and newspaper articles. In his opinion, America needed to break away from Great Britain in every way. Politics. Trade. Even in its ways of speaking and spelling.

And he knew just where to start: with students!

Not much had changed in American schoolhouses since Noah was a boy.

Students did not learn *American* geography.
They did not learn *American* history.
They did not read *American* stories by *American* authors,
if they had any books at all.

~Class of 1779~

I taught at several schools after I graduated from Yale, and that's how I got my first book idea.

And not one school used an *American* dictionary with *American* words, like *skunk*. No, American students had to use *British* books.

Old ones too.

Bah!

Reading *American* books could help "unshackle" America's young minds from Britain's "haughty" grip, Noah argued.

Noah also wanted to help students learn to read.
And reading, he believed, began with *spelling*.

A wild idea back then.

A...m...e...r...i...c...a...n...

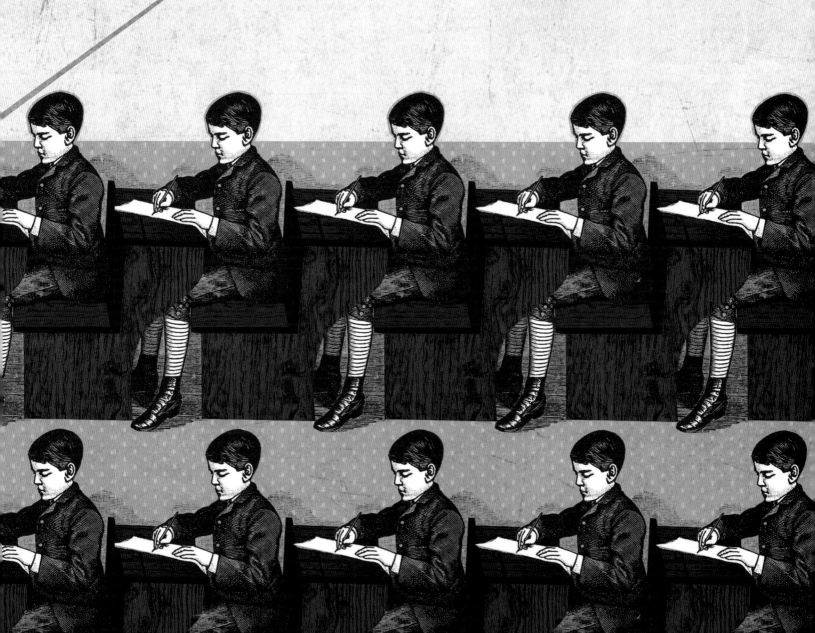

Noah published *A Grammatical Institute of the English Language* in 1783, the same year that the Revolutionary War ended.

Later, we wisely renamed it the American Spelling Book.

In his blue-backed speller, Noah grouped words that sounded alike.

He broke words into syllables and used accent marks to show how Americans really said the words.

en'joy!

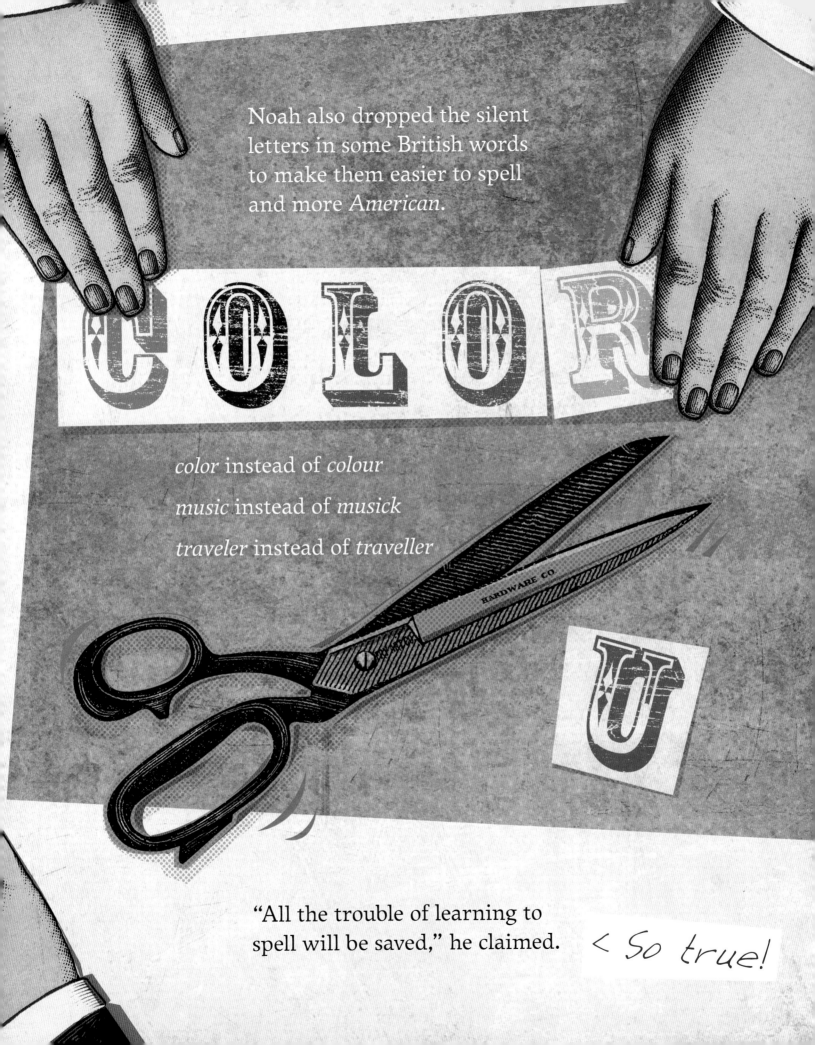

Noah also dropped the silent letters in some British words to make them easier to spell and more *American*.

COLOR

color instead of *colour*

music instead of *musick*

traveler instead of *traveller*

U

"All the trouble of learning to spell will be saved," he claimed.

< So true!

Noah's spelling book became America's first best seller. In the next two years, he added the *American Grammar* and the *American Reader*.

He featured the works of *American* authors in his books, including George Washington.

After he finished his first set of books, Noah looked for more ways to separate *American* English from *British* English.

In 1786 he wrote to Benjamin Franklin suggesting that they work together on a new American alphabet.

Franklin had already invented six new letters. He kindly shared them with Noah.

Yes, THAT Benjamin Franklin!

Their work made sense to them, but the two patriots decided the new United States wasn't quite ready for that much change.

So, Noah worked harder than ever to make spelling easier.
He argued for spelling each word the way it sounded.

  center instead of *centre*

  jail instead of *gaol*

  iz instead of *is*

  riter instead of *writer*

  hed instead of *head*

He argued in speeches.

He argued in essays.

He argued at dinners.

Noah argued A LOT.

But no matter how right *Noah* thought he was, not all of his spellings caught on.

Noah was still confident, of course. He asked the US Congress to make laws for his spellings, so that citizens would spell and speak the same way from state to state to state.

Congress refused.

~~Behind his back, people called Noah "the Monarch" for his bossy attitude. The press said he was an "incurable lunatic" and a "spiteful viper." Noah often lost his temper when someone disagreed with him. He did not take criticism well.~~

Noah was sure America needed its own language. In 1806 he wrote a small dictionary with 40,600 entries. He dropped some of his unpopular spellings from his past work and added truly American words.

chowder, hickory, skunk

He was among the first people to insist that a dictionary must change along with the way people use language.

Many people disagreed. They thought a dictionary should set the rules for using proper English no matter how people actually spoke or wrote. Critics fired more attacks at Noah after his first dictionary was published. One even called him a "literary puppy."

Whatever that meant.

But Noah believed in his ideas. Next, he launched his biggest project of all: a complete dictionary of the American English language.

He built a curved desk in his study to hold about twenty dictionaries and grammar books from different languages. He could turn from book to book to book as he traced each word's history.

With seven busy children in his home, Noah also packed his workroom walls with sand to block out noise while he worked.

In the project's early days, Noah's children sometimes found candies tucked into his study for them.

By the time *An American Dictionary of the English Language* was published in 1828, Noah had begun hiding treats there for his grandchildren.

No one, not another author, scholar, or even a king or queen, has ever successfully changed the spellings of as many English words as Noah Webster did for the new nation.

(I'm blushing!)

Noah's dictionary was the first in a long line of American English dictionaries. Today a dictionary named after him is still published in America—with new words in every edition.

∧ Just the way I knew it should be!

Noah Webster, jun. Esq.

You're welcome. —N.W.

Author's Note

For years, the *Webster's* dictionary on my desk has answered my writing questions. It's one of my most trusted books. But until I saw an online article mentioning Noah Webster's 250th birthday, I hadn't connected the name on my dictionary with a particular individual. Webster immediately intrigued me. How could one person know the spellings, pronunciations, and meanings of all the words in the English language? Why would anyone write an entire dictionary? Who had that kind of ambition and time? I had to learn more about him.

My research took me to Connecticut to see where Noah grew up. I read stacks of books and sifted through the archived materials at Yale University and the New York Public Library. I wondered what Noah would say about his life's work and the way we use English in the United States today. Would he approve of *website* as one word? Would he *LOL*? As I wrote about him, I pictured him reading over my shoulder, quite ready to point out errors or add comments. That's when the idea of Noah editing this book struck me.

Noah had worked as an editor, so he truly fit the role. He had also argued via newspaper editorials with a "ghost" who criticized his *American Speller*. Yes, the Noah I'd come to know would certainly scribble on my manuscript, if he could.

While Noah's ghost is fictitious, all of his comments here are based on what biographers know about this bold, passionate, and visionary patriot. I imagine that Noah would be tickled at the chance to write again. And I'd be honored to share my pen with him.

Illustrator's Note

It's always a challenge when I have to portray a historical figure such as Noah Webster, especially in a children's book.

"Will I be up to the task?" was the first question that came to my mind when I read the manuscript. Other questions immediately followed: How can I bring to life a person who lived over two hundred years ago, make him feel contemporary and likable to kids, and still stay true to the historical setting? How will I manage to keep children visually interested when depicting the exploits of a man who fought not with a weapon but with words and whose battlefield was a mere wooden desk? How can I create dynamic compositions with characters in rather static postures?

I finally opted for a collage style that incorporates realistic elements including some period drawings of objects, created over one hundred years ago by anonymous artists (thank you!), as well as excerpts from period books, newspapers, and Noah's original handwritten letters. To contrast with the realistic elements, I used a lighter approach in the rendering of the characters, aiming for an unexpected and hopefully amusing effect. Thankfully, Tracy's wonderfully crafted text, full of original details, offered lots of opportunities for interesting visual interpretations.

The work is done, and I'm still wondering if I was up to the challenge, but now that's something only the book's readers can decide.

P.S. This note was written with the help of my own *Webster's* dictionary, a trustworthy friend ever since English became my second language. Here's to Noah Webster, my BFF!

Timeline

1758: Noah Webster is born on October 16 in West Hartford, Connecticut.

1774: Noah begins his studies at Yale College in New Haven, Connecticut.

1775: The American Revolutionary War begins. Noah plays the flute for George Washington as the commander marches through New Haven on his way to Boston, Massachusetts.

1777: Noah and his father and brothers try to join the Battle of Saratoga in New York, but by the time the Websters arrive, the Americans have already won the battle.

1778: Noah graduates from Yale College.

1783: The Peace of Paris officially ends the Revolutionary War.

Noah writes the *American Spelling Book*, which was originally called *A Grammatical Institute of the English Language*. Total sales have been estimated to be as high as 100 million copies.

1786: Noah sends a rough draft of his plan for a new American alphabet to Benjamin Franklin, who has a similar plan. Franklin wants to remove the letters *c*, *j*, *q*, *w*, *x*, and *y*, and add six new letters for all English words—not just American words.

1787: The Continental Congress drafts the constitution in Philadelphia. Noah claims the ideas for it came from his 1785 pamphlet, *Sketches of American Policy*.

1788: Noah moves to New York to start the Federalist paper the *American Magazine*.

Noah helps start the New York Philological Society "for the purpose of ascertaining and improving the *American Tongue*." The members listen to his lectures on Monday evenings. They also promote his spelling book.

1789: Noah marries Rebecca Greenleaf on October 26. Over the years, they have eight children: Emily, Frances Juliana (who was often called Julia), Harriet, Mary, William, Eliza, Henry (who died as an infant), and Louisa. The last four of his eight children are born while he works on his dictionaries.

Noah publishes *Dissertations on the English Language*.

1790: Noah publishes *Collection of Essays and Fugitiv Writings*.

1793: Noah founds New York's first daily newspaper.

1800: Noah is elected to the Connecticut legislature and serves until 1807.

1801: Noah begins work on a small dictionary, which is the basis for his major dictionary.

1805: The ninth edition of Samuel Johnson's *A Dictionary of the English Language*, a book Noah owned and used, is published. It contains about 58,000 entries.

1806: Noah releases his first significant dictionary. It has 40,600 words.

1807: Noah begins work on his large dictionary.

1812: Noah moves his family to Amherst, Massachusetts. He helps start Amherst College.

1822: Noah moves his family back to New Haven, Connecticut.

1823: Noah receives his doctor of law degree from Yale.

As a sixty-fifth birthday gift to her father, Harriet commissions the popular portrait artist Samuel F. B. Morse, also a Yale graduate, to paint Webster's portrait. Morse later led a team to develop the telegraph system and Morse code, changing long-distance communication in the United States and around the world.

1825: Noah finishes his dictionary in Cambridge, England, in January. It will take another three years to set and proofread the type.

1828: Noah's dictionary is published in two volumes in November. It has about 70,000 entries.

1843: Noah dies of a lung illness in New Haven, Connecticut, on May 28 with a copy of his *American Spelling Book* in his hand.

After Noah died in 1843, brothers George and Charles Merriam bought the unsold copies of Noah's 1841 edition of the dictionary from Webster's heirs and the right to publish Noah's work. The new owners kept the dictionary growing and changing as Noah intended. Today *Merriam-Webster's Collegiate Dictionary* has more than 165,000 entries—more than double Webster's original large dictionary.

Sources

The quotes in this book, listed in the order they appear, come from the following sources:

"I began life . . ." Letter to the editor of the *Palladium*, February 17, 1835, in Harlow G. Unger, *Noah Webster: The Life and Times of an American Patriot* (New York: John Wiley & Sons, 1998), 113.

"No book for reading" and *"roguish tricks"* Noah Webster, quoted in Unger, *Noah Webster*, 9.

"Unshackle" Ibid., 54.

"Haughty" Noah Webster, "On Education," *American Magazine*, December 1787, 22.

"All the trouble of learning . . ." Noah Webster, letter to Timothy Pickering, May 25, 1786, in Unger, 112.

"The Monarch" Ebenezer Hazard, letter to Jeremy Belknap, August 27, 1788, Belknap Papers, Massachusetts Historical Society, cited in Jill Lepore, introduction to Arthur Schulman, *Websterisms: A Collection of Words and Definitions Set Forth by the Founding Father of American English* (New York: Free Press, 2008), 6, also cited in Luisanna Fodde Melis, *Noah Webster and the First American Dictionary* (New York: Rosen, 2005), 8.

"Incurable lunatic" Benjamin Franklin Bache, quoted in Unger, *Noah Webster*, 205, also cited in Lepore, introduction to Schulman, *Websterisms*, 12.

"Spiteful viper" William Cobbett, quoted in Unger, *Noah Webster*, 221, also cited in Lepore, introduction to Schulman, *Websterisms*, 12.

"Literary puppy" Ebenezer Hazard, quoted in Melis, *Noah Webster*, 8.

"Blockhead" Ebenezer Hazard, quoted in Unger, *Noah Webster*, 44, also cited in Lepore, introduction to Schulman, *Websterisms*, 23.

"For the purpose of ascertaining and improving the American Tongue" *American Magazine* (April 1788), 347, quoted in Jill Lepore, *A is for American: Letters and Other Characters in the Newly United States* (New York: Alfred A. Knopf, 2002), 16.

Selected Bibliography

Of more than eighty additional sources consulted, the following materials were especially helpful in understanding Noah Webster and his life in early America:

Ferris, Jeri. *What Do You Mean? A Story about Noah Webster*. Minneapolis: Carolrhoda Books, 1988.

Ford, Emily Ellsworth Fowler. *Notes on the Life of Noah Webster*. New York: Privately printed, 1912.

Kendall, Joshua. *The Forgotten Founding Father: Noah Webster's Obsession and the Creation of an American Culture*. New York: Putnam, 2010.

Lepore, Jill. *A Is for American: Letters and Other Characters in the Newly United States*. New York: Alfred A. Knopf, 2002.

Lynch, Jack. *The Lexicographer's Dilemma: The Evolution of "Proper" English, from Shakespeare to South Park*. New York: Walker, 2009.

Melis, Luisanna Fodde. *Noah Webster and the First American Dictionary*. New York: Rosen, 2005.

Micklethwait, David. *Noah Webster and the American Dictionary*. Jefferson NC: McFarland, 2000.

Morgan, John S. *Noah Webster*. New York: Mason/Charter, 1975.

Schulman, Arthur. *Websterisms: A Collection of Words and Definitions Set Forth by the Founding Father of American English*. New York: Free Press, 2008.

Shea, Pegi Deitz. *Noah Webster: Weaver of Words*. Honesdale, PA: Calkins Creek, 2009.

Unger, Harlow G. *Noah Webster: The Life and Times of an American Patriot*. New York: John Wiley & Sons, 1998.

Primary Sources

Noah Webster wrote the following books and articles that provided insights to creating this book:

An American Dictionary of the English Language: Intended to Exhibit, I. The Origin, Affinities and Primary Signification of English Words, as Far as They Have Been Ascertained; II. The Genuine Orthography and Pronunciation of Words, According to General Usage, or to Just Principles of Analogy; III. Accurate and Discriminating Definitions, with Numerous Authorities and Illustrations: To Which Is Prefixed, an Introductory Dissertation on the Origin, History and Connection of the Languages of Western Asia and of Europe, and a Concise Grammar of the English Language. New York: S. Converse, 1828.

A Collection of Essays and Fugitiv Writings. On Moral, Historical, Political and Literary Subjects. Boston: I. Thomas and E. T. Andrews, 1790.

An Examination into the Leading Principles of the Federal Constitution Proposed by the Late Convention Held at Philadelphia with Answers to the Principal Objections That Have Been Raised against the System by a Citizen of America. Philadelphia: Prichard & Hall, 1787.

Elements of Useful Knowledge. Volume I. Containing a Historical and Geographical Account of the United States; For the Use of Schools. 6th ed. Hartford, CT: Hudson and Goodwin, 1815.

The New York Directory for 1786: Illustrated with a Plan of the City, also Changes in the Names of Streets, Prefaced by a General Description by Noah Webster. With David Franks. New York: H. J Sachs & Company, 1905.

More Information

Merriam-Webster Word Central
http://www.wordcentral.com/
This is Merriam-Webster's online dictionary for students and others. In addition to looking up words, you can check out the word of the day, play games, and more.

Noah Webster and America's First Dictionary
http://www.merriam-webster.com/info/noah.htm
Read more about Noah Webster and find out more of the things that make him such a distinctive figure.

Noah Webster House & West Hartford Historical Society
http://www.noahwebsterhouse.org
Find out more about Noah Webster and his house, which is now a museum. A "Kid's Corner" offers information about Noah, his family, life in colonial times, and activities.